Motherhood is...

poems by
Jessica Jocelyn

Motherhood is...

Copyright © 2025 Jessica Jocelyn
All rights reserved. No part of this book may be
reproduced or used in any manner without the
prior written permission of the copyright owner.
ISBN: 979-8-9908686-1-8

edited by: Shelby Leigh

For the ones who made me a mother.

-

You are my favorite poems.

Motherhood is...

magical / 1

hard / 33

forever / 73

This book holds deep, honest reflections on motherhood, including the heartbreak of pregnancy loss (pages 49-59) and the weight of mental health struggles. If you find yourself hurting, please know you are not alone. Reach out for support. Your pain is real and your healing matters. Be gentle with yourself as you read.

Motherhood is...

magical

Motherhood is…

Motherhood is…

Between Realms

With each breath,
I alternate between worlds:
one foot in the present
and one where you wait for me.

With each surge of pain,
my body disintegrates
and I am with you in the quiet dark,
where time comfortably doesn't exist.

When the contraction eases,
I return to the present in my body,
still clinging to you
and connecting our worlds.

Nothing matters but movement.
Movement of my breath.
Movement of your body.
Movement of my blood to keep us both alive.

Closer and closer we inch
until one final push
brings you into my arms,
into a world where we both belong.

Lessons for Me

I pour seeds into my son's hands,
his laughter rising as ducks gather
hungry and eager.

His laughter illuminates
everything in childhood I had forgotten.

He sees things untouched,
pure and simple.

He lives in this moment,
grounded by happiness,
having no anxiety about the world around him.

To see the world through his eyes is such a gift,
one that I had dropped along the way.

What a beautiful relationship we have,
where I teach him how to move forward
while he reminds me
to hold on to what matters most.

Motherhood is…

At First Sight

I never believed in love at first sight.
Not until I saw you.

And there I was,
submerged in a love like I'd never known before.

I'd been holding in a breath for nine months,
exhaling all the doubts and fears.

Your hand may have been wrapped around my finger,
but little did I know,
you already had me wrapped around yours.

Motherhood is…

I know love exists because I gave birth to it.

I know miracles happen each day
because I watch them unfold.

I know there is still good in this world
because I see it in their eyes.

Motherhood is…

I know
there is still
good in
this world
because I see
it in
their eyes.

Motherhood is…

The moment I met your eyes,
I knew I'd never be the same.
Love took over,
shaking me to my core.

Nothing else mattered.
Not my past, not my failures.
I would not break,
not as your mother.

With your warmth against me,
I became who I was meant to be.
I left my old self behind
and stepped into forever.

Motherhood is…

As soon as your eyes close,
I am told to put you down.
They say I will spoil you
by giving in to what you want.
But your life right now isn't just
about what you want—
it's also about what you need.
You don't want to control me,
but you need to feel safe.
My warmth and scent comfort you
and my heartbeat is your personal lullaby.
You will never be this small again
and tomorrow you will be even bigger.
So for now, right here in my arms
is where you'll be.

Motherhood is…

This world can be so ugly sometimes,
but still you find a way to make it beautiful.

The days are so long,
but you fill them with joy.

This is the hardest job I've ever had,
but you make it the most rewarding.

Motherhood is…

Your breath slows and steadies
and I can tell you've fallen asleep.

Your head is nestled under my chin
as you lie on my chest.

Tomorrow, you turn one.
Tomorrow, I also turn one.

One year of being you,
one year of being a mother.

Together you and I celebrate
a year full of tears,
of fumbling and figuring each other out.

One year of making it through together.

Tomorrow, you will no longer be a baby,
but you will always be
the love of my life.

Motherhood is…

I will always love you
each and every day.
Even when you're big
because little you will not stay.

Your feelings are so vast
while your body is still so small.
Please, my love, don't be afraid.
I am here to catch you if you fall.

Let the tears flow freely;
don't be scared to scream and shout.
I am your safe space;
that's what being a mother is all about.

I will always love you
each and every day.
Even when you're big
because little you will not stay.

Motherhood is…

I Would Do It All Again

I'd endure every contraction
knowing you'd be at the finish line.

I'd relive every sleepless night,
every minute I spent crying in the shower
from my aching body.

I'd go through the uncertainty of breastfeeding,
remake every bottle with only one hand.

Because you are
and always will be
the reason
I keep putting
one foot in front of the other.

Because of You

Because of you,
the littlest things don't go unnoticed.
From the tiniest bugs on the sidewalk
to the clouds making shapes in the sky.

Because of you,
I see colors of all new shades,
each one more vivid than the last.

I get to experience holidays in all new ways
and feel the enchantment once again.

Because of you,
I get to remember childlike wonder
and question everything about life right along with you.

Because of you,
life is magical.

Motherhood is…

Because
of you,
life is
magical.

Motherhood is…

Pictures of Us

I take pictures of us
for the future version of you
that will no longer have me.

One day, your children will ask,
and you'll see our smiles,
hear our laughter.

You'll remember fun summers
with melting popsicles,
and winters full of snowmen
always with a carrot nose.

I take pictures of us
to freeze the days
when the world was ours.

These Are the Toddler Days

Learning how to be a human days.
The stomping for independence days.
The sudden strength of five grown men as they arch their back so you can't buckle them in days.
When everything is sticky and sometimes you're scared to ask why days.

Days of feeling every emotion possible,
of small hands reaching for you followed by a small voice saying:

"I love you, Mommy."

Days when you watch them sleep
and already miss them.

You might be tempted to wake them, but then they move slightly and your breath catches.

Better to tell them in the morning,
you think, turning off the light.

Motherhood is…

They Call Me a "Girl Mom"

But I had no idea there would be so much sass. And opinions. And more sass. A tiny version of myself learning all about the world with brand new eyes.

There is glitter and pink and magic. Singing and dancing and princess dresses, followed by rain boots, and mud puddles.

Pretend play that I never seem to get the rules right for. Braids and ponytails that always come undone with her wild spirit.

There is strength and independence beyond her years.

They call me a "girl mom" but I just prefer to say a little girl has my heart.

Motherhood is…

When the house is quiet and dark,
there is a small light to guide me as I tidy the living room.

The reset of my day.

My arms are tired; my eyes scream for sleep.

I pick up a miniature teacup I stepped on and place it in my daughter's dollhouse.

I pause.

Small critters sit at a tiny table,
enjoying their tea and cakes.

I can hear her small voice in my head
as she mimics the conversations they must've had.

How they shared stories and treats,
the precious little scene just ready for her to return.

How sweet and innocent she is.
I wish I could freeze this moment,
her imagination untouched by time.

Motherhood is…

Just Like You

If you ever have children,
I hope they are just like you.

I hope you rediscover the magic
in your creativity,
and stand face-to-face
with your unique sense of humor.

I hope you recognize yourself in them,
in their quirks and laughter,
and in the way they make your house feel like a home.

If you ever have children,
I hope you're lucky enough
for them to be just like you.

Motherhood is…

If you ever
have children,
I hope
they are
just like
you.

Motherhood is…

My Middle Baby

Too big to be little,
too little to be big,
always trying to find where you fit.

You are a rhythm all your own,
never too much,
just perfectly you,
teaching me patience along the way.

You reach for the oldest,
while guiding the youngest,
not anyone's shadow,
but a bright light all your own.

I see you.
You are not lost, not least.
You are the glue,
the heartbeat,
the bridge connecting us all.

Motherhood is…

They Call Me a "Boy Mom"

But I think what they mean is there are loud noises and dirt. (So much dirt.) There are stitches and broken bones and laughter. (So much laughter.)

There are sports and video games I do not understand. Being scared half to death as they jump off things and being smothered in kisses.

There are holes in the knees of jeans and grass stains that take some effort to get out. Clothes keep getting bigger and bigger and one day you'll wonder when they started smelling like that.

They start saying things that will make you feel ancient as you Google what they mean.

(And when on earth did I go from Mommy to Bruh?)

They call me a "boy mom" but I prefer to say that a boy has my heart.

My Oldest Baby

The one who knew me younger and brand new.
There were tears and mistakes
and lessons learned the hard way.

My oldest baby.
The one who taught me how to love
in ways I never thought possible

My oldest baby.
The one I watched grow
foot by foot,
moment by moment.
The one who grew while
watching me grow as well.

My oldest baby.
Forever my first,
forever my teacher,
forever my heart.

Motherhood is…

My first baby.
Forever my first.
Forever my teacher.
Forever my heart.

Motherhood is…

I never knew it was the "last time"
until it had passed.

I didn't know the last time
I'd see the newborn scrunch
or the last time you'd let me rock you to sleep.

I didn't realize that it had been months
since I carried you to bed from the couch,
your small body heavy with sleep.

If I had known it was going to be the last time,
I would've savored the newborn scrunch.
I would've rocked you a little longer instead of
rushing through the bedtime routine.
I would've walked you more slowly, more tenderly,
the final time I carried you to bed.

You don't realize how much
you'll ache for each phase until it's gone.

Motherhood is…

Home

Home isn't just walls or windows,
but the hearts within them.
It's all the love and laughter,
the reason I always find my way back.

Motherhood is…

My Husband's Eyes

Our love is brand new. Your eyes are so bright and full of excitement. I've learned they dance when you laugh and crinkle just slightly when you've told a bad joke. Our faces are fresh with youth and plenty of sleep. Your eyes meet mine and in that moment we are connected. We are nervous for the future but our solace comes from the same shared and excited uncertainty in our eyes.

I look at you again and suddenly you're older. There are kids running between us and a sink begging for you to unclog it. There's so much loud madness going on as the baby starts to cry. There's a blow out situation and your eyes meet mine and in that moment we are connected. Our solace comes from the shared helplessness in our eyes.

I look at you again and you're even older. Silver glistens in your hair and wrinkles line your face. They tell stories of all the times we've laughed and even all the times we've cried. Our world is quieter yet filled with more laughter. Grandchildren play in the yard as I watch the sunset cast shadows on your face. Your eyes meet mine and in that moment we are connected. Our solace comes from the quiet agreement that it was a life well spent.

Motherhood is…

Our solace
comes from the
quiet
agreement that
it was
a life
well spent.

Remind Me

Remind me on those days,
the ones that seem to last forever,
when time stretches and patience thins,
remind me that it's okay.

Remind me on those nights,
when our eyes meet in the moonlight,
mirroring the others' exhaustion,
remind me that someday
we will sleep again.

Remind me in the car,
when your hand reaches over
and gently rests on my thigh.
A small touch that reassures me
we're in this together.

Remind me when we walk past each other
and your hand reaches out and grazes my arm
as if to say *I see you.*

Remind me that we've got this.

The Last Baby

There's something about the last baby. You weren't expecting them at all and wondered if you'd be able to handle the unknowns.

And then one day there they are, not just adding to the chaos, but adding to the love, expanding it in ways you didn't know were possible.

The last baby is the one you never expected, but now you can't imagine your family without them.

Their firsts are your lasts.
You hang on to each milestone just a little longer, clinging to the moments you know quickly become memories.

The last baby is your reminder that love can grow in unexpected places.

Motherhood is…

.

Motherhood is...

hard

Motherhood is…

Motherhood is…

Here's to the Mother

She's the one behind birthday parties
and the magic of Christmas Day,
staying awake long after everyone has fallen asleep,
creating memories for her children to wake up to.

Here's to the mother.
The keeper of traditions old and new,
the voice of bedtime stories
and a professional monster chaser.

Here's to the mother.
The healer of everything
from scraped knees to broken hearts.
The tamer of everyday chaos,
making it all seem easy.

Here's to the mother.
Last to go to sleep and first to rise—
the silent, yet strong, foundation.

Motherhood is…

My Village is a Ghost Town

My village is a ghost town.
The streets are silent
and the only voice I hear
is the echo of mine.
The doors are all locked
and no one is home.

Not only is there no one to share
the weight of responsibilities,
but there is no one to help celebrate
the milestones and love.
There's no cheering in the stands beside me,
no phone calls to see how we are.

I want to find this village everyone speaks of,
where mothers are held and cherished
and a shoulder to cry on is not far away.

My arms are heavy and ache
from building everything on my own.
As I wipe the dirt and sweat from my face,
I step back and feel a tiny hand slip in mine.
A small reminder that even though it's hard,
I am enough.

What if it's Not Love at First Sight?

I was promised a flood of emotions,
a love so instant, so intense.
But what if all I feel
is this new weight of the world,
heavy and suffocating?

What if my heart just needs more time?
A love that grows slowly
like roots in dark soil,
a love that doesn't strike like lightning
but instead whispers softly
through the long, sleepless nights?

What if I won't be enough
because I must teach myself
what everyone else says
comes so naturally?
What if I stumble and fall
while my heart is still finding its way?

Motherhood is…

There is a sentence in motherhood that brings both relief and sorrow:
This season will pass.

End of an Era

My daughter tells me she's too big to wear princess dresses anymore. The days of accompanying royalty to the grocery store are now over.

Her collection now hangs in the back of my closet.

As I touch the pastel dresses, I wonder if she got to wear them enough or if I had said "no" too often.

I tell others I'm saving the dresses just in case she has a daughter someday. But in reality, I think I just want to hold on to a piece of her as I slowly say goodbye to the end of an era.

Motherhood is…

To become a mother is to wake up.

I could say I healed myself,
but it was my children
who placed the thread in my hands,
who showed me where the stitches should be.

They held up the mirror,
revealing the cracks,
the parts of me that needed to be fixed.

I will spend the rest of my life
forever indebted to them.
Not for saving me,
but for showing me how.

Motherhood is. . .

I have lost many versions of my children.

I have lost the sweet, sleepy newborn that only seemed to come alive at night.
The cuddly toddler that demanded to do everything themselves, even when it ended in a mess.
The fearless little soul who let go of my hand and walked into their first classroom without looking back.

And in quiet moments, it hits me.
The version before me now will one day be gone too, leaving only memories of this fleeting phase.

My heart mourns each version I have lost,
then mends itself just enough
to welcome the next.

Hellos and goodbyes
and all the beautiful moments in between—
I guess that's what motherhood is.

Motherhood is…

There is a pile of baby clothes that sits in a corner. They are washed and neatly folded. I lightly touch each piece, remembering the times you wore them.

I bring tiny pajamas to my face and breathe deep. The mixture of sweet baby and soap remind me of long nights when it was just us two.

What do I do with these tiny garments? Do I donate them? Do I sell them? How do I know if I'm ready to let them go?

Will I ever truly know?

Or maybe this is how I'm supposed to feel—devastated as I pack everything in a box knowing I am only halfway ready to load it into the car.

"Maybe just a little while longer," I say to myself as I close the box and walk away.

Maybe the ready feeling doesn't really exist.

Motherhood is…

Breaking the cycle breaks you open.

Every demon you've ever met and every childhood monster you shoved back in the closet comes out to play when you become a parent. They announce themselves in the anger you might feel when your children have age-appropriate tantrums. They appear in the words you swallow that want to instinctively spew out.

Breaking the cycle can feel impossible at times. You will doubt and question yourself at every turn. It is not an overnight fix. It is a long-term goal. It is every single day working towards the end result—making sure your children are treated like human beings.

And no, you won't be perfect. And yes, some days you will fail. But decompress and pick yourself up. Come back to the situation when you are calm and work towards fixing it.

This is all new. You don't know how to navigate this. You are undoing generations of trauma that have been seared into your DNA. Never stop growing together. Repair together. You are rewriting history and sometimes in the thick of it, you won't feel very good inside.
But never stop trying. In the end it will be worth it.

Motherhood is…

Breaking
the cycle
breaks
you
open.

Some Days

Some days are so very hard when you are raising children while healing from your childhood.

But nothing comes close to the feeling of the way they love you just for being you.

Nothing is more rewarding than the opportunity to love them.

Motherhood is…

I am building a legacy
that I may never get to see.

I am planting seeds and watering a garden
that I may never enjoy.

I fight against the current of every lie I've ever been told, the ones seared deep in my body, the ones that tell me to react with anger.

To yell.
To scream.
To belittle.

And it hurts.

Breaking the cycle hurts.

It hurts to realize how easy it is to love.
To protect.
To nurture.

I am mending the wounds of the generations before me.

May my words echo for generations to come.

Motherhood is…

I thought I was never going to meet
the child I could've been
had I been loved.

But I did,
the day I gave birth to them.

And every day, I get to watch them grow and thrive,
giving them the love I once needed.

Motherhood is…

My Why

As I looked into your eyes
and smoothed your hair from your face,
I remembered my *why*.

Why I uprooted myself
from where I was planted.
Why I tore my roots from the soil
and searched for safer ground.

When the guilt starts to creep in,
whispering doubts about leaving so young,
I remind myself
I needed earth to nurture you,
and we couldn't grow
where others were still poisoning it.

Motherhood is…

This grief is isolating.
It's so hard to explain my unborn baby's absence
to people who never even knew of their existence.

How do I answer when they ask
how I'm doing?

If I show them my heart,
they shift uncomfortably, unsure of what to say.

The truth is,
my body has healed,
but my heart never will.

Motherhood is…

I search for you everywhere
and in everything.
I look for you in your brother's eyes
to see if maybe you are there.

Every corner I turn,
I hope you're hiding behind it.
I yearn for a face I've never seen
and long to hold hands I've never touched.

Motherhood is…

I don't know where to go
when there is no gravesite to visit.

There is nowhere to put flowers
or tiny stuffed animals.

There is nowhere to physically go.

So I place a hand over my heart,
feeling the beat that once pounded for both of us.

I can't visit you here,
so I close my eyes
and find you in my dreams.

Motherhood is…

I watch my children run and play and wonder how it would look if there had been one more chasing after them.

How would Christmas look with one more stocking next to the others?

How would my rear-view mirror change with one more pair of eyes staring back at me?

What sort of new books would we have read and what new interests would we have explored?

What would it have all looked like?
Been like?

Beautiful.
I'm sure it would've been beautiful.

But for now, I will live for the beauty in front of me while I wait for the day that my lost little love is returned to me.

Motherhood is…

The thing is,
I really do believe others know
how much I cried that day.

How devastating to know
we can break in a million different ways,
but how comforting to be reminded
that even in our darkest moments,
someone else knows our pain.

Motherhood is…

I'm not sure I believe in the saying
"What's meant to be will be."
Because I was meant to have you.
I was meant to feel your presence,
to soak in your wonder and magic.

But now…
you will always be my most painful what if.

What if you were still here,
still shaping me, still changing me?
What would life look like
if your light had made it into the world?

I will search for you in every shadow,
in every quiet moment,
around every corner.

You are my very own
unfinished symphony.

Motherhood is…

Anchor

I wasn't alone
when our baby left my body.

Your arm around me,
holding me so tight,
as if my sobs might tear me apart,
limb by limb.

You laid me on the couch to rest,
but later, you pulled me up,
knowing I couldn't stay there forever.

You knelt beside me in the tub to wash my hair,
your tears falling just enough
to grieve with me,
but not enough to frighten me.

Now we walk, hand in hand,
carrying the weight of a loss
only we can understand.

Motherhood is…

I hope one day
when this life is over,
I find you.
And although I've never seen your face,
I will know you.

Your small body will sink into my arms
and we will smile
as you whisper in my ear,
"I have been waiting for you."

Motherhood is…

We will smile
as you
whisper in
my ear,
"I have been
waiting for you."

The Due Date

Your due date came and went,
a fleeting moment,
a date once circled on the calendar.

And then it came again.
And again.
And again.

A simple number no one remembers,
but the mother.
She is always keeping score.

Motherhood is…

You will always be connected.

Parts of your children will forever flow and nestle
in your body and bits of you will always reside within
them.

A secret exchange,
not just between you and your children who walk this
earth,
but even with the babies
you cannot touch with your hands
yet still feel with your heart.

You are forever intertwined with them.
Even the precious souls born quiet.
For the rest of your life, they will always be with you.

Motherhood is…

Have you ever heard the sound
of a pregnant woman's heart
as it falls to the ground and shatters?

There is no louder sound.
Yet she remains a sight to behold,
gathering the broken pieces,
carrying the weight of her sorrow,
all while still creating life.

She will never forget
how she was treated.
Her screams will echo in her heart,
a melody for her unborn child.

This is why she must be cared for.
Because in caring for her,
you are caring for her baby too.

Motherhood is…

If you knew me before my children were born,
I regret to inform you that you do not know me anymore.
The destruction was violent,
but it had to be.
I lost myself piece by piece.
But brick by brick,
I built someone better.

A Mom's Thoughts at Bedtime

I think I yelled too much / Did I remember their vitamins? / I didn't play with them enough / Does she have practice tomorrow? / Oh no, what happened to that one hoodie? / I hope they aren't getting sick / I forgot to check over homework / I need to pick up dog food in the morning / I need to drink more water / The kids need to eat more vegetables / I should make a chore chart / I'm so tired / I don't want anyone to touch me / Oh, their snuggles are the best / I miss them when they're sleeping / I should peek in on them / No, I need to go to sleep / Oh wait, I can finally start that show / The kitchen is such a mess / I can't sleep / Am I a bad mom? / I love my children so much /

Motherhood is…

She keeps mothering even when she is tired.
When she hasn't had much sleep.
When the coffee has run cold or when it sits in the microwave forgotten for the third time.
There is no number for her to call in when she is sick.
She keeps mothering when her heart is broken.
When her tears only come in the shower,
when the grief is too heavy.
She keeps mothering even when she wants to give up,
because love never lets her quit.

Motherhood is…

The Family Picture

You see them all there—the smiles,
the coordinated outfits.
Perfectly aesthetic and pleasing.

What you don't see is what it took to get them there.
The mother who picked out and planned outfits,
choosing a time that she got everyone ready for.

She was the last person to get ready,
hiding the exhaustion under her eyes
riding in silence
while lost in her thoughts.
Unseen battles heavy on her mind.

Behind her smile,
she carries the nights when only the moon was awake
to see her tears.
This isn't just a family picture.
It's also a collection of stories she doesn't tell.

The mother in the family picture
is the keeper
of the weight of the world,
and the glue
that holds it all together.

Motherhood is…

The mother in
the family picture
is the keeper
of the weight
of the world
and the glue
that holds it
all together.

Motherhood is…

Hidden Rage

They speak of love
but forget to speak of the rage.
They don't tell you that you'll carry
more than just the weight of your baby.

A quiet anger simmers,
building into a sudden explosion
without any warning.

I float through the house like a ghost,
carrying the heaviness of needs
that are not my own.

I didn't know love could feel like a cage,
losing myself day by day.
Sometimes I forget I exist
until I hear a tiny voice call me "Mom."

What is this new fire inside me
that makes me feel like a stranger in my own body?

Is this what it means to love so much it burns?

Motherhood is…

Heavy Expectations

The world expects me to glow
but maybe it's hiding in the deep bags
that have formed under my eyes.

Or maybe it's something I keep in my pocket
and pull out in public when someone recognizes me.

I can't disappoint the ones who cheerfully chirp,
"Isn't it everything you ever dreamed?!"

And I can't let the ones win who stare and say,
"Wow, she really let herself go."

Motherhood is...

I step into the dark
and I meet my postpartum self.

It's 2 a.m. Dirty diapers pile up by the bassinet.

She shushes the baby, but sleep refuses to come.
Tears slip down her cheek, unexpected proof that she isn't as empty as she feels.

I kneel before her and hold out my arms.
"I know, I know," I whisper.

I pull her in, holding her as she sobs.
"It won't be this hard forever. You are doing such an amazing job."

She looks up, tear-streaked, wanting so badly to believe me.

I gently take the baby from her arms and tell her to go to bed, that I will take it from here.

Her eyes dart from side to side, anxiety gripping her body tight.

I touch her cheek; she startles.

"Will I ever sleep again?" she asked.

I laughed softly and reassured her that she would.

Her eyes filled with sudden sorrow as she softly asked, "Am I enough?"

Motherhood is…

My eyes filled with tears.

"You are and will always be enough. No one can love this baby like you can."

She sniffled and gave me a soft smile, hoping one day to fully believe those words.

One day, she'll believe it. I know she will.

Motherhood is…

If I Hadn't Stayed

If I hadn't stayed,
if it had all been over that day,
I wouldn't have seen you take your first steps
or learned your favorite lullabies.

If I hadn't stayed,
if it had all been over that day,
I would've missed your first day of school
and all the stories you told me when you came home.

If I hadn't stayed,
if it had all been over that day,
I would never have realized how beautiful this
journey could be and how full my cup could get.

If I hadn't stayed,
if it had all been over that day,
I wouldn't get to turn around and show other
mothers that they can make it too.

Motherhood is…

There was a time I forgot myself
and felt like I had been reduced to crumbs
scattered all throughout the house.
I got lost in the endless giving
and all the sleepless nights.

Maybe I let my spark dim
not because I wanted to,
but because I thought I had to.
Motherhood had become a quiet surrender,
a love burning both ends of the candle
until I no longer saw any light left.

One day the fog started to clear
and I saw a faint light,
a glimmer of who I used to be.
It grew bigger powered by the laughter from my
children and the way I began to claim moments for
myself even when the world said I shouldn't.

Slowly, my spark returned,
but in a different way.
Steadier, brighter.
It's fueled from parts I used to be and new parts
I have become.
It led to a fire in my soul,
a fire that doesn't just keep my children warm,
but me as well.

Motherhood is…

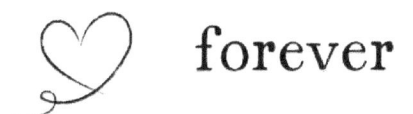

Motherhood is...

♡ forever

Motherhood is…

Motherhood is…

I'm excited to watch you grow,
but it hurts I only get to do it once.
Every single day you are growing.
Jumping.
Playing.
Learning.
Tomorrow you won't be the same
as you are today.
I try not to blink;
it goes by so fast.
Thankfully I know
babies aren't forever,
but motherhood is.

I Was There

I was there when my baby took their first breath,
heard their first cry, felt their first touch.

I was there
in the middle of the night,
soothing every cry, cooling every fever,
chasing away every nightmare.

I was there
on the first day of school,
waiting anxiously,
ready to hear every detail.

I was there
for the homework, the tears, the heartbreak.
For the moments big and small.

I was there.
And I always will be.

Motherhood is…

Motherhood from Scratch

Motherhood has felt a lot like baking from scratch:
gathering the ingredients,
reviewing the recipe,
tweaking it so it comes out better next time.

I was given perfect little souls,
but it was up to me to help shape them,
to "bake" them with care.
I added discipline,
took the time to sprinkle in education.
What didn't work one day
meant trying a new approach the next.

It was all about finding the perfect balance,
though love was the one ingredient
I could never stop adding.
What is too much love anyway?

As they grew into themselves
and began to carve their own path,
I dusted the "flour" off my cheeks
and took a step back.

And there it was,
all the hard work and love
staring right back at me.

Even as they stepped into adulthood,
they'd reach out a hand

Motherhood is...

and tell me they wanted me
to have a place in their life.

In the end, that's how I knew
I had done it right.

Motherhood is…

This House Remembers

Time rewinds when the house tells its stories.
The floors recall the sound of small feet
toddling over them
and the tiptoes of teenagers coming home past
curfew.

The kitchen table has stains that speak of a time when
paint and crayons were once a constant.

The children have outgrown these four walls
but their laughter still echoes from room to room,
songs of who they were
before the world left its mark.

The past is not gone.
It lingers as a quiet memory
safely tucked
into the walls of the house's heart.

Motherhood is…

Every child will discover their path.
It may take them longer than others
but they will get there.

It may not look the way you envisioned
it would,
and your heart may ache
when they face difficulty in finding their people.

In their own time,
on their own path,
what they build will be beautiful.

How lucky are we to witness the journey?
And how privileged to be able to guide it.

Motherhood is…

A Lifetime Ahead

My daughter's eyes close
as she grips her plushie tight.

She has no idea yet,
but there is a lifetime of love ahead of us.
Long car rides full of adventures,
Tears cried and lessons learned.
Dance parties and conversations
shifting well into the night after broken hearts.

She has no idea yet,
but there will be moments when she is angry
and pushes me away,
though I vow to always be easy to find.

She has no idea yet,
but my love will quietly follow her
even when I physically can't.

She has no idea yet,
but we have a lifetime of love ahead of us.

Links

I hope my children realize
that siblings are flowers from the same garden,
trees from the same forest,
fruit from the same vine.

No one else will know the soil
they grew their roots deeply into.

No one else will know the stories by heart
and smile at the same memories.

In the end,
even after I have returned to the stars,
when moments feel uncertain,
it will be just them.
Bound by love and those shared roots,
forever linked by the love we shared.

Motherhood is…

You Won't Remember This

You won't remember this,
not the way that I will.

You won't remember the first time
we were skin to skin,
the first bottles,
and first solid foods.

Your mind won't remember this,
but your body will.

This love, this security,
will nestle deep in your bones.

It will anchor you,
a silent strength in your foundation,
even if you never know it's there.

Motherhood is…

So I Stay

Her days are full of loud shrieks of
"I will do it myself!"
and bold independence.
But her nights,
they turn into whispered fears
and small pleas of
"Mama, please stay!"

I slip into bed next to her.
I whisper that I love her
but she is already asleep.

I listen to her steady breaths
and wonder if at one time,
I was looked at the way I look at her.

She'll never know what she's done for me
just by existing,
but I think that is the whole point.

So when she asks if I can stay,
I stay.

Motherhood is…

She'll never
know what
she's done
for me
just by existing.

Motherhood is…

I come from a long line of women
without a voice—
women contained,
meek as lambs.

When their sadness took all it could,
their anger became a shield,
one they never learned how to lay down.

And then my daughter came.
Loud. Fierce. Unafraid.
She cannot be caged.
She roars like a lion.
She is free to simply be.

She is everything I could have been.
Everything the women before me could've been.

Her voice carries all of our wishes,
so they carry on long after we've gone.

Just Know

Just know that if life should part us suddenly
and I return to the earth,
my final days were made so full
simply because you existed.

Just know that I loved you
long before we met
and you were the sweetest dream
that ever came true.

Just know that you filled my days
with laughter and smiles,
jumping from lava,
and chasing away monsters under the bed.

Just know that the greatest joy
I ever experienced
came from being your mother.

Just in Case

I'm told that I did my job.
I guided you through childhood
and now you're going off into the world.

The muscles in my arms beg my brain
to make them move.
My legs ache to run after you.

You turn your head to smile at me
as I watch you leave.

I say goodbye to the version of you
that lived in this house.

But I will always keep the light on
just in case
you need to return.

Motherhood is…

But I
will always
keep the light on
just in case
you need
to return.

Motherhood is…

The Rocking Chair

There is a rocking chair
with creaking springs.
The padding is worn
but in a comfortable way.
It remembers the mother's body,
welcoming the familiar shape each night.

The stains tell its history:
spills from milk,
newborn spit up,
and even tears shed
when it was just them two.

There is a rocking chair with many miles on it.
It has welcomed new babies
and said goodbyes to toddlers
who became too big for laps.

Many bedtime stories were read
while dreams began
and tiny children drifted off to sleep.

Now, that same rocking chair
is carried out of the house
and loaded into the back of a truck.

A new journey will begin
with new babies to soothe
and a new mother to comfort.

Motherhood is…

The mother watches it leave her driveway
and blows it a kiss
as one tear slides down her cheek.

To her, it isn't just a rocking chair,
but a holder of memories,
an old friend who witnessed
tender seasons of her life.

Motherhood is…

On Your Graduation Day

The funny thing about life is you spend your childhood trying to rush it and race towards adulthood as fast as you can. And then when you reach it, you will try to grasp on to your childhood and yearn for it back.

The younger you and the older you will someday meet and realize they have always been a part of each other. You will get lost in the nostalgia together.

And what is nostalgia
but proof that you have
a life worth living?

I hope when you look back,
you see the love that always surrounded you.

Everyone sees you as you are now.
You are grown and tall,
going off to do big things with your life.

But I don't see what they see.
I see the small baby that was placed on my chest,
all warm and brand new.

They may see you as you are now,
but you'll always be my baby.

Motherhood is…

The Biggest Evidence of Time

In a mother's kitchen,
bottles turn into sippy cups,
then colorful cups with straws.
(Make sure not to pick the wrong one!)
One day, without noticing,
you're washing plain glass again.

Silverware starts off plastic and chunky,
easy to hold,
and then one day it's all silver again.

The pantry is not immune to time either,
from puffs to Goldfish to protein bars.
Colorful snacks soon start to phase out.

The fridge that was once filled
with string cheese and chocolate milk,
now holds containers of meal-prepped dinners.

A mother's kitchen always changes
but it never stops being full of love.

Motherhood is…

Inside this body there is a mother,
though I am not just a mother,
but also a woman with a name.
There are things that make me cry
and even more that make me laugh.
Underneath the shield of motherhood,
I can be soft and vulnerable
in a world that tries to callous me.
My children are such a huge part of me,
but I will always be me.
Before and after them,
I will remain.

Motherhood is…

Before and
after them,
I will
remain.

Motherhood is…

No Better Way to Say I Love You

The room was dark and my husband was asleep. It seemed the only other ones awake in the world were the nurses that randomly came in and out. You were so new with life and exhausted from your arrival. Skin to skin, my warmth transferred to yours. And in that moment, there was no better way to say, "I love you."

Soon you were holding your head up and soaking in the world around you. Crying came less and coos came more often. You stopped nursing and unlatched. Our eyes met and you gave me a gummy smile. In that moment, there was no better way to say, "I love you."

And then you were three and you were running in the backyard. You were either on a jungle safari or a mountain expedition. You tripped and fell and my kisses quieted your tears. A brightly-colored Band-Aid was chosen and you melted into my embrace. In that moment, there was no better way to say, "I love you."

And then one day you were tall. Time passed by in seconds. Your belongings were packed in boxes that filled your car. The drive ahead of you was long and I asked if you already got gas.

You laughed and rolled your eyes and said, "Yeah, Mom, I gotta go."

Motherhood is…

My heart ached at the thought of you leaving and not seeing you every day. But this was what I had prepared you for. I didn't want to let you go, but I knew I had to. You left my arms and got into your car.

It hurt letting you go, but in that moment, there was no better way to say, "I love you."

ABOUT THE AUTHOR

Jessica Jocelyn is a best-selling poet whose work explores love, loss, and the complexities of motherhood. Her poetry, deeply personal yet universally resonant, began as a way to dive into the world of healing and has since touched the hearts of readers around the world. Married and a parent to three children, she finds inspiration in the everyday moments of family life.

instagram: @letters.to.anna
tiktok: @jessica.jocelyn

Motherhood is…

the journey of loving an addict

chasing wildfires

jessica jocelyn

the author's personal journey of the building, destruction, and reconstruction of a family effected by addiction told through poetry.

Motherhood is…

jessica jocelyn

finding
daisies

decorations by
janelle parraz

poetry on healing the inner child
and breaking the cycle

Motherhood is…

jessica jocelyn

encontrando margaritas

decoraciones de janelle parraz

the Spanish version of Finding Daisies

Motherhood is…

girl (remastered)

jessica jocelyn

poetry on childhood trauma, toxic relationships, motherhood, religious trauma, and late autism diagnosis

Motherhood is…

ever・more
POEMS ON PREGNANCY & MOTHERHOOD

jessica jocelyn

poetry on the pregnancy and early
motherhood journey

Motherhood is…

STARS AT LAST

JESSICA JOCELYN

FOREWORD BY ROSE BRIK

poetry on healing from the mother wound
while becoming a mother

Printed in Great Britain
by Amazon